A VERY

MESSY

CHRISTMAS

A VERY MESSY CHRISTMAS

JAGO WYNNE

WITH ILLUSTRATIONS BY CHRIS DENNEMONT

10 Publishing

a division of **10** of those.com

First published in Great Britain in 2021

British Library Cataloguing in Publication Data
A record for this book is available from the British Library

ISBN: 978-1-913896-65-2

Cover design and typeset by Pete Barnsley (CreativeHoot)

Illustrations by Christopher Dennemont

Printed in Denmark by Nørhaven

10Publishing, a division of 10ofthose.com
Unit C, Tomlinson Road, Leyland, PR25 2DY, England

Email: info@10ofthose.com
Website: www.10ofthose.com

1 3 5 7 10 8 6 4 2

For Theo
(as our other three children already have a book
dedicated to them!)

CONTENTS

A TIME FOR JOY?

Christmas is a time for joy.

Whether it's the novelty reindeer antlers or the sprig of mistletoe hanging invitingly from the ceiling; the lights on the tree or the stocking full of presents; the Christmas movie on TV or the glass of mulled wine, Christmas is a time for joy.

I don't know if you have a favourite Christmas memory. Perhaps something about a Christmas in years gone by – either a one-off event or a tradition each year – causes you to smile with that feeling of contented joy. My favourite memory is from my childhood and involves my Grandpa. He was a farmer, and each year we'd all go to stay at my grandparents' farmhouse. If you crammed us all in, it could sleep about fifteen once we had sourced a few extra camp beds. All the family came together, including my brother and three other similar-aged cousins.

We kids would delightedly head out to climb on the hay bales or head up to explore the secret passages in the attic. However, without doubt, the highlight was Santa Claus visiting us in person every Christmas Day afternoon, soon after the Queen's speech had been on TV – a moment at 3p.m. that almost every self-respecting British citizen tunes in for.

Every year, Grandpa went for a quick snooze after he had listened to the Queen, and every year, he sadly missed seeing Santa Claus. Every year, we'd hear the noise of bells from Santa's reindeer, although we never did actually catch a glimpse of the reindeer. But we'd rush to the window of Grandpa's wooden-beamed study, and peer out into the fading light across the garden. And then, with expectation building, Santa would appear from behind the fir tree, carrying a couple of giant, red, felt sacks stuffed full of presents. We'd welcome him in and he'd hand out our presents, bringing us all such delight and cracking the odd joke as he went about his task. Sometimes, Granny would give him a quick kiss, which was a little confusing, and then, with his sacks emptied, he was gone.

Grandpa generally tottered downstairs from his half-hour horizontal about five minutes too late to see Santa.

I may have got older, and possibly even a little wiser about the reality of Christmas traditions, but I still reckon Christmas is a wonderful time for joy. And yet …

1

THE MESS
OF THE WORLD

I have no wish to be accused of being a giant party pooper. I write this whilst dearly looking forward to Christmas 2021, and yet I'm all too aware that the last two years have been a mess for nearly every human on the planet due to the Covid-19 pandemic.

Do you remember the opening scene of the 2017 movie *Paddington 2*? You're transported back in time to when Paddington is a tiny, orphaned bear cub in darkest Peru. You see this drenched, little furry bear clinging onto a log floating down the giant Amazon River. He is fearful and in distress, and understandably so. That journey down the river mirrors how many of us felt over the course of the pandemic.

Uncertainty was all too great a reality. Potential dangers lurked ahead – both in our own lives and as we looked out at the world at large. Each of us had a sense of trying to pick a course through life, but ended up getting buffeted from one lockdown to another, or worse, by the currents of the pandemic.

And whilst the mess of the pandemic may have receded where I live in the UK, due to most people being vaccinated, we're not exactly mess-free. Many predict that a cancer crisis will follow the Covid crisis because so many people missed checks for the disease during the pandemic. When we face up to our own personal concerns about health or finances or relationships, or the more public concerns that are highlighted by the media, our joyous Christmas bubble is deflated all too rapidly. Joy turns to the reality of despair.

It means that if we think about God at all at Christmas, if we think He might possibly exist, then we come to Him with all sorts of questions, even accusations.

Maybe the 'where' question: 'Where are you, God? This world's a mess – it's screwed up. Where are you?'

Or the 'why' question: 'Why is there all this trouble? God, why do you let there be evil in this world?'

Or the 'how' question: 'How can we sort out this world, God? Any chance of a bit of help down here?'

Where? Why? How?

The truth is that these aren't new questions. The Covid-19 pandemic didn't suddenly and surprisingly make us ask these questions for the first time. We've always been asking them. In that sense, the human race has not changed one bit.

About 700 years before the first Christmas, there was a man who was asking these same questions. His name was Isaiah, and he wrote one of the longest books in the Bible. In it, as he tries to navigate a course through the river of life, he cries out to God: '*Where* are your zeal and your might? Your tenderness and compassion are withheld from us.'[1] He can't understand where God has got to, nor why all sorts of bad things are happening in the world. He continues, '*Why*, Lord do you make us wander from your ways … ?'[2] He's saying that if God has made us, then it's God's fault that all this bad stuff happens in the world. He demands that God intervene and sort out all the mess, because humans don't seem to be doing too brilliantly at solving all the problems. '*How* then can we be saved?'[3] he concludes. It sounds all too familiar, doesn't it?

In amongst those questions, Isaiah has one central demand of God. It's a striking request, but one that he knew would silence all his concerns and doubts. One clear way for God to answer all the barrage of questions that were rising up from Isaiah, and from the rest of humanity. This was Isaiah's plea to God: *'Oh, that You would tear open the heavens and come down.'*[4] Isaiah knew deep in his soul that God breaking out from the distant confines of heaven and coming down to be with us on earth was the only way to sort out all the mess.

Just as people do today, Isaiah and his contemporaries thought that the bubble of this world was completely sealed and couldn't be broken. Yet the Christian claim about the first Christmas is that God burst the bubble, broke the seal, tore open the heavens, and came down.

2

THE MESS
OF CHRISTMAS

The first Christmas was a right mess.

The truth is every birth has some degree of mess. Without wishing to overshare, when one of our four children was born, there were a few complications in the labour ward and it was touch and go as to whether the doctors would need to perform an emergency caesarean on my wife, Susannah. But then, all too hastily, our daughter decided to make an entry into the world at a rapid pace. I had to dive and catch her like a rugby ball to stop her from landing on the hospital floor. It was quite literally a hospital pass.

I remember the head midwife on the ward coming into our room about twenty minutes after the birth. Standing there with her hands on her hips, surveying the scene, and tutting her tongue against the roof of her mouth, she uttered the immortal line: 'This looks like a war zone.'

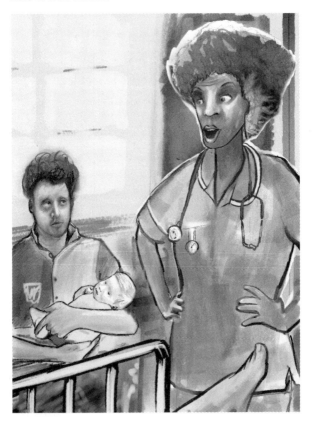

We don't know the exact birthing details for Jesus, but we can safely assume that despite the idyllic Christmas card scenes, Jesus' birth wasn't all cosy and nice. There was no hospital, no midwife, no anaesthetic to help relieve the excruciating pain. It would have been very messy – possibly even resembling a war zone. Then, once the baby Jesus was born, He was placed in a manger – an animal's feeding trough.[5] Jesus was literally born into the mess.

And the mess wasn't just in the manger.

There was social mess. Mary and Joseph were pledged to be married, but not actually married, and yet the bun was well and truly in the oven. Culturally, this would have been disastrous. Mary would have been socially ostracised by her community for being pregnant outside of marriage, but this wasn't the most messy part of it. The bigger problem was that Joseph himself knew that he was not the father. Put yourself in Joseph's shoes – what a mess. The perceived betrayal and the humiliation would have been unbearable. Until an angel appeared to Joseph in a dream, telling him that the baby was conceived from the Holy Spirit, Joseph had been planning to quietly call off the wedding.[6] And whilst the dream changed Joseph's outlook on the whole affair, I imagine that many others would have believed that an affair was exactly what had taken place.

On top of the social mess, there was also the societal mess. Caesar Augustus had just issued a decree that a census should be taken of the entire Roman world.[7] This census was for taxation purposes and was organised by the Roman Empire for all the nations over which they had control. As every person had to head back to their home town to be counted, it meant huge, enforced upheaval and travel for so many. The society into which Jesus was born faced oppressive restrictions, was fearful of the future, and had the challenge of an uncertain journey back to normality.

Jesus is no stranger to the mess we experience today. He was born into a right mess.

3

THE MESS-IAH
OF CHRISTMAS

The solution to mess often comes from places you least expect it. Think of Paddington in that messy and dangerous situation on his log, heading down the Amazon River, about to career over the waterfall. Where is his rescue going to come from?

In the film, the camera pans up from the turbulent river to Aunt Lucy and Uncle Pastuzo, two adult bears, sitting on a rickety old rope bridge that straddles the giant Amazon. As they sit on the bridge, high above the river, their feet dangle down, the sun is shining, and, naturally, they're enjoying some marmalade sandwiches. Suddenly, they spot Paddington on his log. Aunt Lucy, this rather rotund bear, somehow bungee jumps down from the bridge with even more agility than her species namesake, Bear Grylls. With perfect precision, she descends to just above the river. Upside down, and with her hands outstretched towards the foaming water, she plucks this little bear cub from the log, and rescues him into her arms as the log plummets over the edge of the waterfall.

There is more to Christmas than just mess. There is also a Mess-iah. Messiah means 'saviour, deliverer, liberator or rescuer'. The claim of Christmas is that this Messiah figure didn't come in the form of a politician or superhero or vaccine or philosophy, or even as a bungee-jumping brown bear.

Like Aunt Lucy, this Messiah did tear open the heavens and come down. But He came down as a baby. As Sir John Betjeman wrote in his famous poem 'Christmas':

And is it true,
This most tremendous tale of all,
Seen in a stained-glass window's hue,
A Baby in an ox's stall?

The Maker of the stars and sea
Become a Child on earth for me?'[8]

It's like your landlord becoming your lodger, or Beatrix Potter becoming Peter Rabbit. The Creator became part of His creation. Yet it's not just Betjeman who declared this. That first Christmas night, there were shepherds out on the hillside around Bethlehem. They were certainly amongst the lowest-ranking people in society at the time, and probably some of the messiest too. And yet it is to them that God chose to send an angel to announce Jesus' birth. The angel declares, 'Today in the town of David a Saviour has been born to you; he is the **Messiah**, the Lord. This will be a sign to you: you will find a baby wrapped in cloths and lying in a manger.'[9] God's angelic messenger declares that God Himself has landed on planet earth in human form to rescue us.

Like us, those shepherds would have been longing for someone to come and sort out all the mess, doing a rescuing act greater than Aunt Lucy did for Paddington. The most powerful person they would have known about would have been Caesar Augustus. If anyone could bring about lasting peace or make poverty history or stop global pandemics or save the planet or deliver racial justice, then you'd expect the most powerful person to make that possible. If anyone could possibly be a Messiah figure, it would seem to be the one whose full title was 'Commander Caesar, Son of the Divine, Augustus'. But the angel, with his declaration, points the shepherds not to the palace of Caesar, a supposed 'Son of the Divine', but to the manger in which lies Christ, the real Son of God.

The Messiah tore open the heavens and came down as a feeble, messy, mucky baby – dependent on His parents to feed Him and clean Him. Yet this baby grew up to be the only person ever to walk on this earth who could sustain the weight of our hopes and fears, and still never leave us disappointed. The only person who could enter into the mess of our world and begin to rebuild it.

That's because Jesus, being God Himself, is the only One who is without His own mess. He went from the crib to the cross that He might take the punishment for all our mess – both yours and mine – so that our lives might be rebuilt in Him.

I have few claims to fame, but one of them is that I have been the understudy of a famous British pop star. This would come as a great

surprise if you knew me because I am tone-deaf – my voice is far from angelic. My children insist that I stop singing in carol services because they can't bear the drone I make. In fact, when I was ten, I was thrown out of my school's junior choir because, according to the music teacher, my voice didn't 'quite fit in with everybody else's'. Nonetheless, despite my vocal limitations, I was made the understudy for someone who has sold more than 20 million albums, won two Brit awards and was voted Hottest Male in the 2010 Virgin Media Music Awards.

My understudy role was also when I was ten. James Blunt, he of 'You're Beautiful' fame, was the lead part in the Christmas school play. However, two days before the first performance, he decided to swing on a toilet door in the changing rooms, fell off, and got concussed. As a result, I was James Blunt's substitute on the first night of the play. I took his place (and thankfully it involved no singing).

Similarly, Jesus Christ took our place. Jesus is our substitute – not on the wooden boards of a school play, but on the wooden boards of a Roman cross. Each of us should face the punishment of the cross for our mess – all the ways we go through life curved in on ourselves, focusing on me, myself and I, rather than loving God and loving others. So often we take all the gifts of life, but ignore the ultimate Giver. At Christmas, we wouldn't dream of ignoring those who give us a gift, but most of the time, we ignore the One who gives us all our greatest gifts of life and health and a job and family and so much more.

Yet, because of His great love for us, Jesus the Messiah took all our mess on Himself on the cross. As He tore open the heavens and came down to this earth, He went down all the way to the depths of hell for us as He died on the cross. He was our substitute. He faced God-forsakenness for us, so that we never need face it ourselves.

4

THE MESS-AGE
OF CHRISTMAS

At Christmas, there is the Mess, the Mess-iah, and also the Mess-age.[10] The angel shares that message with the shepherds: 'But the angel said to them, "Do not be afraid. I bring you *good news that will cause great joy.*"'[11] I wasn't lying when I wrote at the start of this book that Christmas is a time for joy. We've had the memo from the very top. God says that Christmas should cause us to be bubbling up with great joy because it is a message of such good news.

But why? Particularly why when more than 2000 years after God tore open the heavens and came down, all the mess of this world does not seem to be any more sorted since this supposed Messiah's arrival?

The answer is all to do with birthdays.

The joy of gifts

The first reason is because of the joy of birthday gifts. You can probably remember a birthday of yours that was especially joyful because of a particularly fantastic present you were given. As I track through my life, I think of my Big Ted, my globe, my pogo stick, my rollerblades, my yucca plant, and my giant, furry onesie as presents that have brought me such joy. I also remember the giant present all wrapped up for me for my fourteenth birthday that I thought was going to bring such joy. When I ripped open the wrapping paper of this vast gift, with massive expectation, and it turned out to be nothing more than a dull, brown suitcase, joy was definitely not my overriding emotion. That day I gave a perfect display of how to be a moody teenager.

Often, our own birthdays are all about the joy we receive, but they can also be about the joy we give too. I have deeply enjoyed plenty of other people's birthdays because of what the birthday person gave me, whether that was the party they threw or the meal they cooked. Invariably, the highlight for my children in going to their friends' birthday parties is the party bag they are given as they leave. It is stacked high with a slice of birthday cake, too many fizzy sweets, an annoyingly noisy, plastic wind instrument and a cheap stunt glider whose wing invariably breaks the first time you throw it.

Christmas is all about a birthday – Jesus' birthday. And what we discover is that Christmas is not about what we can give Jesus on His birthday, but about what He has given to us. Jesus has given us Himself – the Messiah who can rescue us from all our mess by taking it on Himself on the cross. This gift is the ultimate good news message that can bring joy to your heart.

The joy of life

Think a little more about why birthdays are joyful. We celebrate the birthdays of people who are alive, not those who are dead. And at Christmas, we celebrate Jesus' birth because He is alive today. The One who died rose again. At the first Christmas, He tore open the heavens and came down, but at the first Easter, He tore open the earth and came up.

If that's true, Jesus rising again and being alive today changes everything.[12] Fundamentally, Jesus' resurrection brings joy because it shows us that He can sort out all the mess of this world.

His rising from the dead shows us that His death on the cross was effective in paying the price of all the mess of our sin. It worked. He paid the price so that we don't have to do so. This world does still currently contain all sorts of mess as a result of human sin – both ours and other people's. However, because of Jesus' resurrection, we can have certain hope that there will come a time when He will bring all those who are trusting in Him to a place free from all mess – a place where we will have sin-free bodies in a sin-free world. In the Bible, this is described as a place where: 'There will be no more death or mourning or crying or pain, for the old order of things has passed away.'[13]

Particularly after the Covid-19 pandemic, we all yearn for this future. I don't know about you, but I'd love to experience a mess-free world like that, and the wonderful news is that one day we can. If Jesus rose again, then He overcame death, which is the ultimate symbol of mess. A fear of death is the one thing that most destroys joy. And death is the one thing that has more obviously come into our consciousness recently with the pandemic, whilst being the one thing that none of us can ultimately avoid.

Our youngest child, Theo, is the one out of our four children who has shown the most desire to be independent when little. He is currently five, and he always likes to do things by himself, without any help from anyone else. He has this bold (or foolhardy?!) confidence that he can do anything. This has included finding him trying to drive our car out of our driveway by himself; watching him run across the beach to the sea to go surfing by himself; climbing trees by himself; taking his older brother's skateboard to the skatepark by himself; and, most recently, discovering him in the kitchen chopping up vegetables with a sharp knife by himself.

Most of the time, Theo doesn't like us holding him or helping him. He thinks he can go it alone. Yet, even with Theo, when we do venture somewhere that is completely out of his comfort zone – such as going on the London Underground for the first time – he slips his little hand into mine faster than you can say, 'Mind the Gap'. He knows there are times that I can help him navigate what is scary and unknown to him, because it is not scary and unknown to me.

All of us are searching around for a guide to take us through the scary and unknown thing called death, and Jesus Christ is the one person who has got Himself through death and come out the other side to tell the tale. He is the only guide whose hand is worth holding as we face death. This Messiah has the power to bring about a mess-free world *and* He has the power to lead you through death to be there. This is the second reason that the message of Christmas is good news of great joy.

The joy of names

One of my dearest friends from university is called Bayo, and he is Nigerian. I'm godfather to his eldest son, Tobi, and I also had the great privilege of conducting the naming ceremony for his second boy, Tayo – short for Olutayo. When the day came for the naming ceremony, just a few days after his birth, what I didn't realise was how many different names Tayo would be given, all of them in the Yorùbá language. I had to read out about twenty different names.

Whilst Bayo has always been very kind about my efforts, I am sure I mispronounced nearly all of the names! But here is the striking thing: nearly every name they gave Tayo was about declaring joy. Olutayo itself means 'God is enough for joy'.

The Messiah was not born that first Christmas with quite so many names, but all His names also give a reason for joy. First, starting with His most well-known name, this Messiah was called Jesus. The angel who appeared to Joseph in a dream said Mary 'will give birth to a son, and you are to give him the name Jesus, because he will save his people from their sins'.[14] The name Jesus is the Greek form of Joshua, which means 'the Lord saves'.

As you and I look back on our own lives, in amidst the good times there are things in the past that we will each regret and feel shame about. The wondrous news is that this Messiah came to deal with our past and save us from our sin and wrongdoing. Where we should know condemnation for our sin, we instead receive no condemnation despite our sin.[15] Jesus has paid for it on the cross. The name Jesus tells us that we can know *God's pardon for the past*, and that is good news of great joy.

Second, the Messiah was to be called Immanuel, which we are told means 'God with us'.[16] Many people today, and you may be one of them, say they struggle to believe in various parts of the Christian faith – such as the miracles or that one man's death could deal with all our sin or that Jesus really did rise from the dead. But all those struggles stem from not grasping the most remarkable claim of all – that this baby in the manger was truly God with us on earth.

I struggled to believe that as a teenager. Then, aged seventeen, and just before Christmas, a friend encouraged me to go with him on a Christian conference for people aged sixteen to eighteen. I had thought Jesus was irrelevant, and that God, if He existed, was a distant deity who was out to spoil my fun. But as I read the Bible, heard talks about Jesus, and discussed it all with others, I discovered something extraordinary – that Jesus was 'God with us'.

As I read of Jesus calming the storm, I could see God's power.[17] As I eavesdropped on Jesus' conversation with a woman who had had five husbands, I could see God's compassion.[18] As I pictured in my mind Jesus turning over the tables in the temple, I could see God's righteous anger.[19] As I analysed Jesus' death on the cross, I could see God's love.[20] As I encountered the baby in the manger, I could see God. The invisible God became visible to me in Jesus. I discovered that Jesus is God with us, and that changed my view of God. I no longer saw Him as a remote deity on a par with a gruff headteacher dishing out punishments to stop us having too much fun. Instead, I recognised God for who He is: the One who loves us so much that He came to be present with us and share all the experiences of our lives – the One who we can know present with us even today by His Spirit. The name Immanuel tells us that we can know *God's presence for the present*, and that is good news of great joy.

Third, the Angel Gabriel told Mary that this Messiah was to be named 'the Son of the Most High'. He explained the reason for this name concerned the future: 'He will be great and will be called the Son of the Most High. The Lord God will give him the throne of his father David, and he will reign over Jacob's descendants for ever; his kingdom will never end.'[21] The message of Christmas is an invitation to join the kingdom of the Son of the Most High – Jesus' kingdom, which is a kingdom that will never end.

Over the course of the last couple of months, I have been writing this book and also meeting up with someone who had been debating responding to Jesus' invitation to join His kingdom. This person had lived a fairly wild life, been diagnosed with terminal cancer, and had already exceeded the doctor's expectations of how long he would live by six months.

Three weeks ago, we talked together about how Jesus died on the cross with two thieves crucified alongside Him – one on His right, the other on His left. One of the thieves continued to mock this so-called King Jesus for claiming to be the Messiah.[22] The other was the exact opposite. He asked the Messiah hanging next to him to be his King. Through the agony and pain, the second thief cried out to Jesus, 'Jesus, remember me when you come into your kingdom', and Jesus replied, 'Truly I tell you, today you will be with me in paradise.'[23]

As we talked this incident through, my friend with terminal cancer decided to pray to King Jesus accepting the invitation to join His kingdom.

Just like the thief on the cross, he prayed, 'King Jesus, remember me.' It was a wonderful, joyous moment. Straight away, he knew pardon for his sin and a relationship with his Messiah.

My friend didn't join Jesus in paradise that very day like the thief on the cross, but two weeks later he did. He has now joined the Son of the Most High whose kingdom will never end. The name Son of the Most High tells us that we can know *God's paradise for the future*, and that is good news of great joy.

The message of Christmas brings joy and the Messiah's birthday names tell us why. They inform us that because He tore open the heavens and came down, we can experience God's pardon for the past, God's presence for the present, and God's paradise for the future. They are names that can fill us with joy.

But there's still more …

5

THE MESS-AGE
FOR THE WORLD

You might be thinking that this good news brings joy for some people, but it's not for you. It's for religious people or for good people or for people that were brought up Christian. The fact that I've just mentioned my friend who recently died of terminal cancer and the thief on the cross might have caused you to reassess your view. But then again, you might have thought this proves that the message of Christmas is just good news for bad people who are feeling guilty or weak people who need a spiritual crutch or ill people who are about to die.

Well, what does the angel declare to the shepherds? So far, I have purposefully left out four words of what was said on that first

Christmas night. The angel said to them, 'Do not be afraid. I bring you good news that will cause great joy *for all the people*.'[24] This message is for the religious and the irreligious, the good and the bad, the healthy and the sick, the capable and the incapable, those with many regrets and those with few. It is good news for every single person on the planet. The visitors to the baby Jesus demonstrate this to us. The shepherds were poor; the wise men rich. The shepherds were locals; the wise men from afar. The shepherds were Jewish; the wise men pagan. Yet they all knew that this message about a Messiah was relevant to them.

Maybe your fear is that you think you are worthless or too bad or that you don't have anything to offer the Messiah? Well, you can't have less to offer than the shepherds, or indeed the thief on the cross. But what you might find harder to believe is that we don't have more to offer Jesus than this criminal or the shepherds. As the wise men came to Him in their expensive clothing, bringing Him fine presents of gold, frankincense and myrrh, it might have looked like they had far more to offer Jesus. Yet read what took place and you discover that the wise men's first action on seeing Jesus with His mother Mary was 'they bowed down and worshipped him'.[25] Faced with the true King, the first response of these three kings was one of humility and worship. They were willing to take the crowns off their own heads, as it were, and put the crown on King Jesus – their Messiah.

The message of Christmas is a joyous message for the world, but it is also one that cannot be ignored. Though we misplace our trust and misdirect our desires and mistake our abilities to sort things out in our own strength, the truth remains that we still all need a Messiah like Jesus. And it is only our pride that stops us responding to Him.

Dietrich Bonhoeffer was a German pastor who tried to overthrow the Nazi regime in World War Two, and was executed as a result. He knew that we fear some things, such as Hitler, for the wrong reasons, whilst there are other things that we should fear for good reasons. He once said, 'There are only two places where the powerful and great in this world lose their courage, tremble in the depths of their souls, and become truly afraid. These are the manger and the cross of Jesus Christ.'[26]

That's why when an angel appeared to Joseph in his dream, and when an angel appeared to Mary, and when an angel visited the shepherds on the hills outside Bethlehem, each time the angel began with the same words: 'Do not be afraid.'[27] There is someone who it is right to fear because of His awesome majesty. That someone is Jesus.

Bonhoeffer continues,

We have become so accustomed to the idea of divine love and of God's coming at Christmas that we no longer feel the shiver of fear that God's coming should arouse in us. We are indifferent to the message, taking only the pleasant and agreeable out of it and forgetting the serious aspect, that the God of the world draws near to the people of our little earth and lays claim to us ... Who among us will celebrate Christmas correctly? Whoever finally lays down all power, all honour, all reputation, all vanity, all arrogance, all individualism beside the manger; whoever remains lowly and lets God alone be high; whoever looks at the

child in the manger and sees the glory of God
precisely in his lowliness.[28]

The message of Christmas is a message on offer to all the world. There is no one outside of the offer. But the message of Christmas is also a message that needs to be received by all the world. It is only us thinking we don't need the help of a Messiah that stops us. God is in the manger, and we are to bow down and worship Him.

A few years ago, some friends gave Susannah and me a fantastic present. They gave us a colourful box the size of a large book, and told us that inside was a mystery weekend. We were instructed not to open it until the Friday evening of the designated weekend, and that we had to have our passports at the ready.

When we eventually opened the box with huge excitement, having managed not to take a sneak peek beforehand, we found inside some train tickets for the Eurostar, details for a hotel in the centre of Paris, a guide book, and some spending money. There was even a booking for a taxi to pick us up from our home and take us to the Eurostar.

It was one of the most brilliant presents we have ever received. We didn't have to do anything to organise the weekend. Our friends organised it all, and they paid for it all too.

And it's like that with Jesus. He offers every person on the planet not a weekend in Paris, but His pardon for the past, His presence for the present, and His paradise for the future.

Our weekend cost our friends around £600 (roughly $850), but the gift that Jesus offers you and I is worth all the riches of heaven, and is paid for by Him through His death on the cross.

In one sense, Susannah and I didn't have to do anything for our mystery weekend. Our friends arranged and paid for it, and yet we benefited. Yet in another sense, we did have to do something. We could have just left the box unopened.

For every person in the world, Jesus offers us the gift of Himself – a Messiah to deal with all our mess. But He will never force us to accept the offer. He loves us, and love never forces. This Christmas, will we accept Him as our Messiah, the King in our lives, or will we just leave this gift under the tree unopened?

6

THE MESS-IAH
FOR YOU?

As a parent, one of the key moments in the run up to a British Christmas is the nativity play most schools or preschools organise. As much as any parent might say they are not fussed about what part their child has, the reality is very different. At least it is for me.

One year, one of our children came back from their day at preschool to tell us that they had been cast as one of the three kings. 'Not bad,' I thought. 'My boy's a king.' That was better than when one of our other children was once cast as a puddle in their nativity play! But then, a couple of days before the big performance, our son came back to announce that he wasn't going to be a king, but instead was going to be Joseph.

On the outside, I played it cool. But inside, my inner, competitive dad instinct was going into overdrive. Move over Tom Cruise and Benedict Cumberbatch, my son is Joseph!

When the day of the nativity play arrived, I took a couple of hours off work, and strode into the preschool with a bit of a swagger. 'Get out of my way. Front-row seat please – my boy is Joseph. He's the star of the show.'

The play started, and Mary and Joseph came on stage along with a dodgy-looking donkey. But as I peered under Joseph's tea towel, it became apparent that Joseph was not my son, and my son was not Joseph. In fact, as the play continued, I discovered he wasn't even one of the three kings. He was just one of the plethora of angels floating aimlessly around the back of the stage, chatting to their friends, and picking their noses.

Celebrating Christmas can sometimes feel like that nativity experience – a bit short of what we were anticipating. We build up the expectation for a perfect Christmas, only for the reality to disappoint. Have you had a Christmas when everyone is exhausted and irritable because the children haven't slept due to overexcitement

and overindulgence in chocolate, and the day has been full of bickering and tears? I have. Sometimes, when I was the child, and sometimes, when I was the adult.

As I write this in 2021, I wonder if many of us are so desperate to put behind us the Covid-19 pandemic, which stole all our hopes for a perfect Christmas in 2020. Yet the truth is that however much planning and preparation we undertake for Christmas any year, too often the reality will include elements that are a bit of a mess and which fail to satisfy. Our perfect Christmas bauble/bubble always ends up cracked and deflated.

Whilst elements of our Christmas celebrations sometimes turn out worse than our expectations, the actual message of Christmas is always far better than expected. You may not have seen much similarity between yourself and a bunch of shepherds looking after their sheep on a hillside in Israel 2000 years ago. But there is one thing that each of us has in common with them. They were faced with the same dilemma that faces every single one of us in the world: is the message of Christmas true or false? Is the baby in the manger really the Messiah come to rescue us from our mess?

After the angels had left them, we are told that 'the shepherds said to one another

"Let's go to Bethlehem and see this thing that has happened.'"[29] They decided to do some investigating. In a sense, as you have been reading this book, you have been doing just the same. You have been investigating the message of Christmas, and I hope you have seen that it is far better than expected.

Do you remember what Isaiah said? In the face of all the mess of this world, he cried out to God: *'Oh, that You would tear open the heavens and come down.'*[30] He feared that the bubble of this world was completely sealed and couldn't be torn apart, but he longed for God to intervene and enter into this world. Seven hundred years later, at the first Christmas, God responded to the plea of Isaiah. The wonder of Christmas is that in one single event – in a stable round the back of a pub, in Bethlehem, under a starry night, 2000 odd years ago – God provided an emphatic answer to all those 'where', 'why' and 'how' questions:

Where? 'I'm here. God with you.'

Why? 'I'm sorting out all the mess in you and in this world'

How? 'Through being your Messiah.'

I don't know what present you are hoping to receive for Christmas this year. My favourite recent present was some noise-cancelling headphones. They're excellent – not just for listening to music, but also because, with the press of a button, the computerised voice declares, 'Noise cancelling on', and suddenly the world goes silent. Nothing comes in. With the headphones on, my world is undisturbed.

However, all too often we can do that in our own lives. We don't let anything disturb us or challenge us or change us or alter us. We don't let anything come in.

Maybe we hear the message of Christmas now, but then we put the headphones back on and power into the New Year, not allowing the claims of Jesus the Messiah to disturb us in any way. We cancel out the noise of the Christmas message.

At the first Christmas, Jesus tore open the heavens and He came down.

At the first Easter, Jesus tore open the earth and He came up.

My prayer is that today, as you have been reading this book, you might be ready to let Jesus tear open the bubble of your life and come in as your Messiah and King.

Sometimes, bursting a bubble can feel messy. But when we pull off our noise-cancelling headphones and allow Jesus to enter the bubble of our lives, we are flooded with love, peace, care and joy that only the true Messiah can give.

Thank you for reading this book. I hope you have a very merry Christmas. But even more, I pray you have a very messy Christmas as you trust in the joyous message about the Messiah who deals with all our mess.

Here is a prayer that you might like to pray this Christmas:

Dear Jesus

Thank you that you tore open the heavens and came down to earth at the first Christmas.

Thank you for coming as the Messiah to rescue me from all the mess.

I am sorry for all the mess I have caused in this world – by living my life focused on myself rather than on you and others. Please forgive me.

Thank you that you died on the cross to pay the price of my mess.

Thank you that you tore open the earth and came up, proving your victory over sin and death.

Thank you that the message of Christmas is good news of great joy for all people – including me.

Jesus, I open my heart to you. Please come into the bubble of my life as my Messiah so that I might know your pardon for the past, your presence in the present, and your paradise in the future.

Thank you, Jesus.

Amen.

If you prayed this prayer, that is wonderful news! I encourage you to get in touch with the person or church that gave you this book and ask them how you can continue life with Jesus as your Messiah. You might want to join an Alpha or Christianity Explored course that is running near you. Head to alpha.org or christianityexplored.org for more details.

NOTES

1. The Mess of the World

[1] Isaiah 63:15, my emphasis.

[2] Isaiah 63:17, my emphasis.

[3] Isaiah 64:5, my emphasis.

[4] Isaiah 64:1, NASB, my emphasis.

2. The Mess of Christmas

[5] See Luke 2:7.

[6] See Matthew 1:18–20.

[7] See Luke 2:1.

3. The Mess-iah of Christmas

[8] John Betjeman, 'Christmas' (1954).

[9] Luke 2:11–12, my emphasis.

4. The Mess-age of Christmas

[10] Others have used a similar Mess/Message/Messiah motif before me. One I remember is Dai Woolridge in his excellent *Mess*, a Christmas spoken word film produced by Spoken Truth in partnership with the Bible Society.

[11] Luke 2:10, my emphasis.

[12] If you are not certain about whether Jesus really did rise from the dead, why not try reading *The Case for Easter: A Journalist Investigates Evidence for the Resurrection* by Lee Strobel (Zondervan, 2014).

[13] Revelation 21:4.

[14] Matthew 1:21.

[15] See Romans 8:1.

[16] See Matthew 1:23.

[17] See Mark 4:35–41.

[18] See John 4.

[19] See Matthew 21:12–17.

20 See Luke 23.

21 Luke 1:32–33.

22 See Luke 23:39.

23 See Luke 23:42–43.

5. The Mess-age for the World

24 Luke 2:10.

25 Matthew 2:11.

26 Dietrich Bonhoeffer, *God Is in the Manger: Reflections on Advent and Christmas*, compiled and edited by J. Reiss (Westminster John Knox Press, 2010).

27 Matthew 1:20, Luke 1:30, and Luke 2:10.

28 Dietrich Bonhoeffer, *God Is in the Manger: Reflections on Advent and Christmas*.

6. The Mess-iah for You?

29 Luke 2:15.

30 Isaiah 64:1, NASB, my emphasis.

 Publishing

10Publishing is committed to publishing quality Christian resources that are biblical, accessible and point people to Jesus.

www.10ofthose.com is our online retail partner selling thousands of quality books at discounted prices.

For information contact: **info@10ofthose.com** or check out our website: **www.10ofthose.com**